FUTURE CRYPTOCURRENCY IN AUTOMOTIVE

MARTIIN COUTURE

TABLE OF CONTENTS

AUTOMOTIVE INDUSTRY WITH CRYPTOCURRENCY

The automotive company operates in a sequence of processes that can be simplified to summarize in the following stages: innovation, design, manufacture, sale, and maintenance. Each of them, coordinated in space and time, can decompose into linear or matrix processes. If innovation, sales, and maintenance do not proceed from particularly original methods or different from those of other technical professions, design and manufacture (cf. AUTOMOBILE - Manufacturing) is pretty specific in the automotive industry. The challenge is for the manufacturer to develop, every six years (or even much less), an original and complex object, at the cost of the previous one - by improving quality and performance and adapting it to changes in international legislation. -and to reproduce it in large quantities.

THE HISTORY OF THE AUTOMOBILE IN THE TWENTIETH CENTURY

This century is mainly recognized by all the industrialization movements that occurred in the big cities. Therefore, the use of cars was increasing at this time, but their sale was still only for mostly privileged social sectors.

During this century, Peugeot also began its foray into the automotive industry creating in 1891 5 units of Oldsmobile, and in 1899 it managed to assemble 400 cars in just 6 months. A clear example that the numbers were increasing.

In this way, the beginning of the 20th century represented a watershed for the automotive industry at an economic level. In the United States, this industry will become more critical both for society and for the government. Detroit in Michigan was the first capital used by the first companies in the auto industry.

Cryptocurrency is a term that refers to both a digital currency and a peer-to-peer payment system. As a result, these digital currencies are virtual currencies because they lack physical backing: there are no coins or banknotes, and purchases by check or bank card are also not feasible.

Alternative currencies are not accepted as legal tender in any region. Their value is not linked to the price of gold or other traditional currencies, and any central authority or financial institutions do not control them. There are no central banks at the helm of their affairs. And yet, security and transparency are their main assets! Because cryptography secures transactions that are all verified and recorded in a public domain, ensuring both confidentiality and authenticity thanks to Blockchain technology.

Cryptocurrencies are all based on the same concept: the Blockchain. Cryptocurrencies are a sequence of numbers stored in blocks on a disk. The guide is quite simple and mainly well explained in the article published in Bitcoin and cryptocurrencies, new digital coins: "Take a database. Set up a very long and complicated control protocol that must be followed each time a certain number ("block") of changes is requested. Authorize someone to make changes to this database on the sole condition that they declare themselves as a "member." This process is carried out by all of the voluntary "members," rather than by a single controller. Once validated, the "block" of changes is dated and applied to the others in the registry. Finally, allow everyone to read the registry, and you have a blockchain database".

The major cryptocurrencies are built on this technology and structure, but Blockchain implementations go beyond that. Indeed, removing the need for trusted third parties can disrupt the entire financial sector and particular industries such as legal and administrative services. With this distributed register technology, which helps make data safer and more transparent, there is no need for a notarial act or civil status register. After all, blockchain technology is a ledger that can't be altered unless certain conditions are met.

Blockchain technology disrupts the automotive industry, driving the adoption of intelligent technology/cars by cutting out the middleman and protecting data. Blockchain, a technology popular for its application in cryptocurrencies like Bitcoin, is being explored by automakers to improve safety in increasingly connected vehicles. As the average car moves closer to being fully connected and electric and sovereign, there will be a subsequent growth in the need for a more evolved the corresponding database, and the Blockchain looms as the solution.

What precisely is a blockchain, and how does it work?

A blockchain is a distributed database, which means that the storage devices in the database are not connected to a standard processor; instead, It maintains a growing list of organized records referred to as blocks. Since each block has a timestamp and a connection to the one before it, it's difficult to alter one without affecting the others. Users who own the private keys required to write to the file can edit parts of the Blockchain they "have." Cryptography guarantees that the distributed Blockchain is still up to date.

By definition, blockchains are stable databases, making them ideal for storing medical records, financial transactions, identity management, and proof of provenance. Blockchain offers the potential to cut out the middle man in business and transactional processing. Here are five ways Blockchain has become a disruptor and driver of its adoption in the automotive industry

![Mining hardware being configured]

1. **Secure payment in the vehicle**

Blockchain first gained mainstream attention as the technology behind cryptocurrencies such as Bitcoin; Cryptocurrency remains the most popular application of blockchain technology. However, car owners could soon use the Blockchain to pay for electricity to charge electric cars. Imagine if every time you trust your vehicle, the action triggers a smart contract on the Blockchain that takes the appropriate amount of money from your account and sends it to the charging station. The same

could happen with your monthly parking cost, insurance, and any other financial transactions related to your vehicle.

2. Autonomous data protected

As an autonomous vehicle navigates the world, the Blockchain could become responsible for recording data on the details associated with the journey. This location data could include everything from information on road and infrastructure details to general traffic patterns. Other vehicles on the network could then access this information and trust that since it has been processed using blockchain technology, it is accurate and secure (the data structure of the ledgers shared on blockchains makes adding, removing, or altering data almost impossible once it has been validated and stored in a block). Since sharing everyone's data is the fastest path to autonomous driving, automakers could soon take advantage of the Blockchain to share all location data in the most secure way possible. Only authorized parties could access this data in real-time because it is cryptographically secure. Hacking is big business and not as much of a threat to individuals as it is to OEMs. Using blockchains will prevent "bad actors" from hacking into the network and potentially holding OEMs hostage due to a rollout of what can be done with the automaker's autonomous vehicle network.

3. Decentralized shared transport

Transportation network services like Lyft and Uber are already reinventing the way we use (or don't use) our vehicles. With a few swipes in an app, a driver picks you up in his car and drives you to your destination. Blockchain, coupled with autonomous technology, could take carpooling to the next level in the not-too-distant future. One of the Blockchain goals is to eliminate intermediaries between the passenger and the driver while establishing more secure data maintenance. Drivers will be charged only after delivering a passenger to their destination by basing payment on predetermined conditions and encoding them in a smart contract. If a passenger cancels, the agreement could release a small portion of the funds for the driver to account for their time, rather than an arbitrary cancellation fee. There's even the potential for blockchain technology to disrupt the way companies as Uber operates. An ecosystem-type framework could be designed to remove the middleman by moving payment processes and selecting driver/passenger to the Blockchain, which is impartial and safe. Passengers may use such a platform to communicate directly with drivers, display individual reputations, and select a driver based on price, quality, and other market factors. Many drivers fed up with the existing ride-sharing payment system associated with companies like Uber will be a welcome option.

4. Fair and reliable carpooling

Not only do blockchain-based systems make it simple to share rides, but they also make it simple to share vehicle ownership. A group of people may, for example, pass vehicle ownership in the future. Instead of each person living in an apartment tower having their car or depending on other means of transportation, they could share a fleet of 10 vehicles. They would request access to a vehicle when they need it through an app, and during use, the car's Blockchain would record the activity of each vehicle.

The system would automatically settle payments on the basis that owners agree, and the secure nature of the Blockchain would take the guesswork out of how long, how far, and how fast the vehicles were used, which would ultimately turn out to be more. Convenient for everyone.

5. Supply chain management

The transparency offered by distributed ledgers in the automotive industry will help ensure that manufacturing, shipping, and suppliers all see the same supply chain, rendering counterfeit component insertion virtually impossible. Additionally, multiple blockchains could be used to manage the massive amounts of data generated and monitored daily by automotive manufacturers and suppliers: one Blockchain could store vehicle part loading lists. At the same time, another could keep quality inspection records. Another could store WIP details for each vehicle assembly from start to finish during the manufacturing process.

Smart contracts may also be incorporated in industrial blockchains to release purchase orders automatically at specific stages of the manufacturing process. Automatically awarding contracts to the supplier with the most comprehensive available inventory may help supply chains.

6. The possibilities seem limitless.

The Blockchain, as a secure and unique form of encryption, has the potential to be one of the critical technologies that enable the automotive industry to move into the new era of intelligent vehicles. Whether it's protecting financial information or making shared ownership more trustworthy, Blockchain has the potential to transform how data is handled in future cars, and it's worth keeping an eye on.

How Cryptocurrency and Blockchain Are Transforming the Automotive Industry

Mobility Open Blockchain Initiative (Mobi) is a nonprofit organization that includes automotive giants like BMW, General Motors, Ford, and Renault and businesses in the technology, finance, and insurance industries. "It's about building trust in a business network between parties, which would not otherwise be transparent," said Ballinger.

Industry executives have expressed their excitement at the prospect of the new technology. "We believe that Blockchain will transform the way people and businesses interact, creating new opportunities in mobility," explained Rich Strader, vice president of mobility product solutions at Ford.

The announcement, which has taken a year to build, comes from the hands of at least a halfdozen auto industry titans who are announcing forays into blockchain technology. Although most of these ventures are still in the early stages, Ballinger and his group work toward a common goal: Blockchain will revolutionize the auto industry if used correctly. The industry is very likely to look wildly different in a decade from today.

Building an Ecosystem

Ballinger started playing with blockchain technology when he was head of innovation and new mobility at the Toyota Research Institute.

He began to see a move towards on-demand mobility whereby infrastructure was pay-as-you-go rather than buying new cars. "I started to think that in that world, distributed blockchain ledger was the perfect fit because the infrastructures of these cars need to communicate," Ballinger explained. "They need ways to make automatic payments, pay for usage, pay for congestion, pay tolls, pay for energy as they go, and have secure identities for both the car and the passengers."

The Toyota Research Institute introduced proofs of concept that used blockchain technology to answer these issues under his supervision. Although they were popular in theory, the idea did not take off.

"I began to understand that this was not at all uncommon," Ballinger said. "I kept seeing major corporations placing assets on the blockchain, announcing it publicly, and then letting it die."

The purpose, according to Ballinger, is that there was no ecosystem to help those ideas flourish. "If there is nothing else on the network, the technology alone is useless," said Ballinger. «It is like email or fax in the day; If there is no one to email or fax to, your fax machine is just a good stop. And so, building the ecosystem was the fastest step it took.

Ballinger claims that "The automotive industry, as well as how customers purchase, insure, and use cars, is poised to be redefined by Blockchain and related trust-enhancing technologies. We will boost adoption for the benefit of companies, customers, and communities by bringing together automakers, suppliers, entrepreneurs, and government agencies."

Dive

There seemed to be a new announcement about an auto giant dabbling in blockchain technology every day in the first few months of 2018.

Ford, for example, obtained a patent in late March to use cryptocurrency and blockchain technology to enable cars to communicate and, in some cases, pay each other while on the road.

But the patent, according to Karen Hampton, originally from Ford Motor Company, is not necessarily indicative of a current product plan. Instead, it symbolizes the company's ability to experiment with new concepts. "Patent applications are meant to shield new inventions, but they aren't always a sign of new company or product plans," Hampton said.

Audi revealed a few days later that it explored blockchain technology for its physical and financial delivery systems, intending to improve supply chain security and transparency. Porsche is collaborating with Berlin-based startup XAIN to investigate the use of blockchain technologies in its cars. BMW is also rumored to be expanding its portfolio by working with British startup Circular to phase out battery minerals made with child labor.

Perhaps the most advanced in developing a car-based use for Blockchain is Mercedes Benz, which currently tests its MobiCoin app to reward drivers for environmentally conscious driving. MobiCom uses blockchain technology to link a smartphone app with Mercedes-Benz vehicle technology that tests how "green" the vehicle is driving. Drivers can win "coins" via the app based on how green their car is gone, which can be exchanged for prizes like VIP tickets to high-profile events like the MercedesCup final.

"The **MobiCoin** technology is an experiment to discover how technology can influence behavior," said Jonas von Malottki, senior manager of finance and control solutions at Daimler, which owns Mercedes. "We wanted to make something that was car-centric and incentivized for eco-driving," says the designer.

And, even though von Malottki had several people explaining to him how the organization could use Blockchain, it became clear that they weren't the correct methods. "For [MobiCoin], we have a currency behind it, so it was good to use blockchain," he explained. "It's the kind of technology that allows us to make it very people-centric, blockchain makes it a lot easier and a lot more reliable."

Mercedes, like the other firms, is still in the development phase; after the two-month trial period is over, it will be determined if MobiCoin will be available globally or not.

Automotive industry experts and blockchain tech experts agree that if automakers don't innovate and make use of Blockchain now, well, they will regret it.

"Times are shifting," von Malottki said, "to more autonomous, self-driving electric vehicles." "We're adjusting to this age, and in order to do so, we're having to change our business model more and more." One of the most exciting technologies for this type of transformation, in my view, is Blockchain.

According to Teodoro Lio, CEO of Accenture and leader of automotive and industrial innovation, From the control of vehicle identification numbers and crash records to the dynamic supply chains that lead to assembly lines and dealers, Blockchain would have a significant effect on the automotive industry. "Industry leaders are beginning to understand the unique characteristics of this technology and its various forms," he said.

According to Derin Cag, founder of Richtopia and co-founder of Marketing Runners and Blockchain Era, companies are jumping on the blockchain bandwagon because of the great opportunity and what will happen if they don't.

"If they do not do it, the competition will do it and destroy a large segment of their business," articulated Cag. "The party that gets it right the first time will change the business as it exists today; the industry will not be the same in five to ten years due to all of the transformations."

The Blockchain has changed the meaning of innovation in cars. From Porsche to Ford, these are the companies that want to revolutionize the industry with Blockchain.

In the blockchain world, car porn takes on a whole new sense. Gone are the chassis and cherrycolored paint jobs, and in their place are projects chasing high transaction returns, tokens to reward environmentally conscious driving, and even self-driving cars. According to this year's Global 2000 list of the world's largest public companies, there are seven exciting projects. Although each is still in the early stages of growth, when viewed as a whole, they provide a clear image of what blockchain technology popularized by bitcoin has accomplished.

A red Porsche 911 GT3 RS car is illuminated under the lights before being shipped from the Porsche AG factory in Stuttgart, Germany. Photo: Krisztian Bocsi / Bloomberg

✝ Toyota

Location: Japan
Sales: $ 265.2 billion
Blockchain Play: The Toyota Research Institute revealed last year that it is collaborating with the MIT Media Lab to investigate how Blockchain could be used to exchange selfdriving car data and details for insurance rates safely.

✝ Daimler

Location: Germany
Sales: $ 193.2 billion
Blockchain Play: Mercedes-Benz issued a 100 million euro bond backed by a private version of ethereum. Then he said in a post - which has been removed - that he tested a crypto token to incentivize safe driving.
This Toyota GT86 is on display during the Vienna Autoshow, as part of the Vienna Holiday Fair. Photo by Manfred Schmid Photo Getty Images

✝ BMW

Location: Germany
Sales: $ 114.4 billion
Blockchain Play: BMW is a founding member of MOBI and develops new ways to track mileage using the Blockchain.
An attendee takes a photo of a Mercedes-Benz AG E300e during the press day of the 2018

Busan International Auto Show in Busan, South Korea. Photo: Bloomberg

✝ Ford

Location: United States

Sales: $ 159.6 billion

According to a patent granted earlier this year, blockchain Play: Ford is exploring cryptocurrencies for self-driving car passengers to use PayPass. Ford is also an established member of MOBI.

An attendee takes a picture of a BMW M4 CS vehicle on display during the 2018 Busan International Auto Show. Photo: Bloomberg / SeongJoon Cho

✝ Renault

Location: France

Sales: $ 66.3 billion

Blockchain Play: This French car giant collaborated with Microsoft and the Video to establish a tamper-proof car registry to verify a car's maintenance history, in addition to being a founding member of MOBI.

A Ford Motor Co. Expedition sport utility vehicle (SUV) is parked outside the Ford Kentucky Truck Plant in Louisville, Kentucky. Photo: Luke Sharrett / Bloomberg

✝ General Motors

Location: United States

Sales: $ 144,420 million

Blockchain Play: In May, GM announced that it helped launch the Mobility Open Blockchain Initiative (MOBI) to accelerate Blockchain adoption, a nonprofit comprised of automakers and governments has formed.

Carlos Sainz of Spain, a Renault driver, drives at the Barcelona Catalunya circuit in Montmelo, Spain, just outside Barcelona.

✝ Porsche

Location: Germany

Sales: $ 38 million

Blockchain Play: This German automaker collaborates with Xain, a Blockchain, and AI startup, to grant temporary access to a vehicle and test new business models based on encrypted data logging.

On the back of a CT6 V-Sport car, the General Motors Co. Cadillac logo is mirrored.

Cryptocurrencies: advantages, risks, and future according to three experts

Jesús Pérez (Director of CryptoPlaza), Jorge Soriano (Co-Founder of Criptan), and Iacopo Piersantelli (CEO of Cryptounify), three experts in cryptocurrencies, answer several questions about digital currencies, a sector that is growing despite its enormous volatility and distrust that they provoke in political, business and financial sectors.

- **Jess Pérez (CryptoPlaza Director):** The Crypto Currency term refers to a digital representation of money based on digital systems that rely on cryptography to ensure its security in transactions and storage. While there were several cryptocurrencies before the launch and adoption of Bitcoin, this word became familiar with the birth and adoption of Bitcoin.

  On the other hand, Bitcoin is the first to store data on a distributed network of computers, making it much more immune to attacks and almost impossible to shut down, much like spread music distribution networks.

- **Crypton Co-Founder Jorge Soriano:** To be honest, I haven't been a part of this ecosystem since its inception. As a result, I've attempted to study and meet others who have done it. I'm left with Murad Mahmudov's description of Bitcoin after all I've seen and learned. I am going to refer to what Bitcoin is, the first Cryptocurrency that arises. "Bitcoin is a new form of money, a new way of thinking about money, about storing it, transferring it, and organizing it. It has over 100 definitions, and many people debate it, but for me, Bitcoin is primarily a new form of money, a new way of thinking about money, about storing it, transferring it, and organizing it. and comprehend it, as well as all of the secondary financial consequences that result from it."

- **Lacopo Piersantelli (CEO of Cryptounify):** Using bitcoin (BTC) as an example, a cryptocurrency is a decentralized digital currency that is represented by a non-duplicable chain of code and exchanged between users through the Bitcoin protocol (commonly called Blockchain). By encrypting data, this protocol ensures ownership and prevents double-spending (that is, duplication). Aside from that, the Bitcoin (Blockchain) protocol also deals with the generation of BTC, or Cryptocurrency, through a reward system directed at miners. They are in charge of validating transactions, adding blocks to the Blockchain (generating new bitcoins), and keeping the network stable with the power of their computers.

What advantages do they have?

There are many advantages compared to digital money. Among these benefits, we will find that they can be sent virtually instantly and at a low price to anyone with an Internet connection, making them a superior technology for foreign money transfers. They also have the benefit of being detachable. That is, no one can take our money away from us.

Bitcoin, in particular, is highly secure since it has never been possible to create new Bitcoins, even though attempts to counterfeit money are continuously made. Another benefit is that, unlike conventional currencies, where states can create more currency, there can never be more than 21 million Bitcoin.

Advantages: It is decentralized: any state does not control it, bank, financial institution, or company.

Bitcoin is governed by standard software installed on thousands of computers distributed throughout the world and is based on the same rules for everyone; no one can change them if the vast majority do not agree. Anyone who does not follow them is immediately kicked out by the rest of the group, ensuring no one can significantly influence the operation. It is deflationary: the number of new bitcoins issued decreases over time and eventually reaches 21 million. In conventional currencies, this eliminates the primary source of inflation. It's fast: you can send any number of bitcoins in a matter of minutes, regardless of the destination. It's cheap: the cost of making a transfer in bitcoins is pennies irrespective of the amount.

You have complete control of your bitcoins: your bitcoins are yours alone. The owner of the BTC is the only one who controls them. No entity can change or prevent transactions or block accounts.

It's safe: forgery or duplication is impossible thanks to a sophisticated combination of proven cryptographic techniques. It is universal and accessible: it can be used all over the world equally. Anyone anywhere in the world can create an account without intermediaries and receive money without connecting to the Internet.

Freedom: for the first time, it is possible to transfer value digitally, make payments without the need for an intermediary (banks, PayPal, etc.) in total freedom, 24 hours, 365 days a year. Ownership: Each cryptocurrency holder is their bank, and this is proven and verified by the cryptocurrency blockchain. There are no intermediaries neither in the transfers nor in custody.

Transparency: every transaction made on a blockchain will always be public. Pseudo Anonymity: the transactions carried out in the chain do not show the data of those who carried them out, but only the address of the starting and destination wallet and the balance of the transaction. However, cryptocurrencies focus on privacy, where this information also tends to be hidden, and solutions such as side chains or coin mix also increase the privacy of transactions. Volatility: the vigorous-intensity of price changes make the cryptocurrency market the best financial instrument in recent years.

Cyclically, speculative bubbles triggered by bitcoin's deflationary mechanism allowed investors to earn huge sums over the years. Unstoppable - No one can block or prevent a transaction on a blockchain. Accessibility: everyone can open a wallet and start sending and receiving cryptocurrencies. Commissions: they are much lower than current systems, especially for sending large sums or foreign transfers.

And what are the downsides?

The main risk they have is that to manage this money, we will have to take care of a long password that will allow us to carry out the operations. If we lose this password, we will not be able to recover the digital money. Another problem is that they currently have a lot of volatility to lose or gain many price movements.

It has high volatility today. Slow development: Many people believe that the growth of Bitcoin is prolonged, but in my opinion, this is a positive thing. We must keep in mind that even the tiniest mistake (and we're talking thousands of lines of code) may be fatal to Bitcoin. Therefore, all the improvements, adjustments, etc., are carried out with great care. Simple UX for users with little knowledge. Regulation: work is already underway on its rule, and there are several European Union directives pending approval.

  + **Volatility:** the intense price changes, on the other hand, have also caused losses, in addition to making the payment with cryptocurrencies such as bitcoin not convenient due to the continuous evolution of its value in local currency, remember the example of pizza paid with 10,000 BTC in 2010 that today would be $ 100,000,000!

- **Fungibility:** the full tracking of bitcoins could lead to complications in the use of centralized services.
- **Commissions:** the cost of commissions is variable based on the "load" of the Blockchain. In times of heavy use, transactions will slow down, and the price will increase, which makes cryptocurrency payments inconvenient for small expenses.
- **Scalability:** the number of transactions that a blockchain can support is minimal compared to the more widespread centralized systems like Visa.
- **Custody:** coins are like cash, so there is no way to get it back if it is lost. If you lose your key to access the wallet, you lose all the balance you had. As for cryptocurrencies held in third-party services, such as exchange houses or other custody services, in the event of an attack by hackers, it will depend on them whether they have insurance or whether users will be reimbursed.

How many are there in the world?

There is some confusion when the world talks about cryptocurrencies because any digital cryptoasset tends to be called. Still, these crypto-assets represent shares of a company or represent a real estate asset in many cases. Cryptocurrencies, that is to say, that only have a purpose of being used as currency. We can talk about 200 cryptocurrencies approximately. Its greatest exponents are Bitcoin, Litecoin, Ethereum, Monero, Bitcoin Cash, Dash, Tether, etc.

According to Coin market cap, today, there are 2368 between cryptocurrencies and tokens, where the vast majority are tokens. This is something essential to take into account. You have to differentiate between token and Cryptocurrency. Broadly speaking, and it could go much more profound, the main difference between a token and a cryptocurrency is that cryptocurrencies use their Blockchain. Tokens use a cryptocurrency's Blockchain to function. Tokens usually have a different function than being "money." They can represent actions, parts of a product, be exchanged for services, etc.

Today, there are hundreds of different cryptocurrencies. If we add to these the tokens created on top of some blockchains that allow their creation, we reach almost 8,000 coins. But we remember that today the most widespread and secure Cryptocurrency is bitcoin. We can also have a dozen leading alternative cryptocurrencies, but that today they do not guarantee decentralization and security at the same levels of bitcoin.

Predictions on the impact of Blockchain

Here are some predictions from industry experts on the impact of Blockchain

Reliable tracking

Blockchain consists of progression blocks of data or transactions across a computer network without a central authority when used as a distributed ledger. This allows logs to be shared between clouds and even between companies without giving a single player the power to modify this.

This has powerful implications, to begin with, the fact that digital assets, identity, credentials, and rights can be stored and shared.

Blockchain can even be used for functions you would never think of, as the Provenance company did, which used it together with clever tags to track tuna from the moment it is caught until it reaches the consumer, allowing the exploitation of this food to be sustainable and verifiable. among other benefits.

Technology disruption

Blockchain technology began to affect the world, not just that of cryptocurrencies, seriously. Even defense contractors in America began exploring cybersecurity options using Blockchain. Thus, it could emerge as a potential disruptor in many industries, first resolving some vulnerabilities until the technology is considered mature to be the foundation of enterprise security.

The term unknown to many

The term bitcoin has been used left and right, even without fully understanding it. The same will happen to Blockchain, which will continue to be a hot topic in 2018. Unfortunately, many will not learn of its full potential beyond its relationship with bitcoin.

A possible solution for security challenges

Blockchain adoption will continue at a higher pace in 2018. This will occur most strongly in the Middle East and Asia. Furthermore, with the increase in ransomware attacks demanding digital currencies, both Blockchain and IoT will emerge on defenses based on cryptocurrency technologies. Likewise, it will help the digital transformation in companies, specifically in the automation and digitization of processes, tokenization of physical goods and activities, and coding of complete contracts.

The insurance sector will also be affected by blockchain technologies. Claim processing and processes involving various players, such as surrogacy, will be an area where Blockchain will show its potential, especially for its help in automation. Security breaches will show the need for a secure blockchain-based approach, where no one has all the keys.

Investment of companies in Blockchain

Blockchain is more than Bitcoin and Ethereum. Many entrepreneurs will begin to brag about the investment they have made in this technology, as well as the apps and products they will launch. The next application of this technology will be ultra-enhanced ledgers or ledgers. Blockchain's ability to enforce transparency and security in each transaction will be shown, altering industries that require the transfer of assets or information with confidence, reducing friction and costs.

Tips for acquiring cryptocurrencies: Trust Corporate

Mexico, Brazil, and Argentina are experiencing an increase in the use of cryptocurrencies in Latin America. The financial consultancy Trust Corporate shares several tips regarding the acquisition of cryptocurrencies, given the recent boom that this market in Latin America recently; derived from the impulse caused by the economic crisis of the pandemic concerning the increase in digital payments and collections.

Through a statement, the consulting firm refers to the Binance Research report, which indicates a 63% confidence in crypto assets; and that 52% of users who have crypto investments see in this area an opportunity to generate more income.

In addition, the company Chainalysis, specialized in the study of crypto assets, is also cited in a survey conducted in 2020, which reveals Venezuela and Colombia as the two nations with the highest use of Bitcoin in the region. Meanwhile, Mexico, Brazil, and Argentina are experiencing an increase in the use of this Cryptocurrency. "Like any investment, it is crutial to know the risks involved in daring to start in the world of transactions with virtual currencies. In the case of cryptocurrencies, there is still a way to go in terms of education, operation and regulation, which must be taken into account, "said James Hernández, president and co-founder Trust Corporate.

In this sense, James Hernández Trust offers four recommendations for those who wish to enter the cryptocurrency market:

1. **Distrust the portals that ensure exponential profits.**
    Many platforms promise users that they will recoup the initial investment with profit quickly with just a tiny amount. "It is always crucial to seek expert advice and be informed. Although these types of assets can represent some type of long-term investment or trading opportunities, it is also true that as more people are interested in cryptocurrencies, You're likely to fall into the hands of scam artists who promise to double your money if you invest in a business."

2. **Not exposing all resources.**
    "We are facing a scenario of speculation and cryptocurrencies are characterized by their volatility. The advice is always to invest in a diversified way; with safer investments and other riskier ones, such as cryptocurrencies. As a result, it is crucial not to use any of your resources or all of your investments to conduct cryptocurrency transactions."

3. **Keep in mind that the Law does not cover you.**
    For the president of the consultancy Trust Corporate, virtual currencies are not yet governed by any regulation, so those who wish to bet on them must be aware of their risks. "Investing in stock or highly volatile assets requires in-depth knowledge of the market and also a full-time dedication, because, just as you can earn a large sum, you can also lose everything in an instant ."

4. **Check local companies that promote cryptocurrencies.**
    There are web portals with malicious content where data theft occurs. "It is essential to read comments and research about companies that promote cryptocurrencies. Something that can help is to check the company in the search engine, the company's name, along with keywords such as 'scams' or 'complaints.'
    Regardless that the cryptocurrency sector is overgrowing, there is still uncertainty regarding the investment opportunity. However, different banking institutions in Latin America have already started pilot tests with crypto-asset trading platforms. According to the

Coinmarketcap report, the cryptocurrency market at the end of February was 61% by Bitcoin, 11.8% for Ethereum, and 2.3% for Binance Coin.

Bitcoin [BTC]: Automotive Industry Proves Blockchain Is Its Guaranteed Future

The adoption of crypto and its underlying technology, Blockchain, is increasingly finding new ways to grow. This time around, auto giants Honda and General Motors (NYSE: GM) are working together to use Blockchain in their intelligent vehicles.

This association aims to see if electric cars can stabilize the energy supply in smart grids. They decided that Blockchain could help them achieve this.

Cryptocurrencies: permissibility risk

Cryptocurrencies have revolutionized the way we traditionally hold and transfer value. Unlike other investment modes or commercial exchanges, cryptocurrencies are not supported by any productive asset, resource, central bank, commercial bank, or government. Its value is governed purely by supply and demand, being a speculative digital instrument.

The always alluring speculation for the potential benefits with low cost and effort has historically been little accepted by the regulated markets. However, an increase in the acceptance of cryptocurrencies has been observed given their popularity, historical volatility, and ease of transaction, generating a significant level of permissibility risk, that is, the acceptance of an excessive tolerance to the inherent financial risk that we would think we would not see at the corporate treasury level.

At the beginning of February 2020, several media publicized the purchase of an amount in Bitcoins equivalent to 1,500 million dollars by a highly recognized technology company, increasing the value of that Cryptocurrency significantly announcing their plans to receive cryptocurrencies. As payment for its goods and services, which marks a milestone in the history of corporate treasuries after the previous transaction of Bitcoin had already generated an active market, as shown below: Transaction - millions of Bitcoins in circulation at the end of each year:
5.0 (2010), 15.0 (2015), 12.6 (2012), 18.4 (2021).

The active market generated by cryptocurrencies has already been recognized and started to be regulated. In Mexico, the Fintech Law of March 2018 recognizes the existence of virtual assets within which cryptocurrencies are considered, instructing Banco de México (Banxico) to issue general provisions for Financial Technology Institutions and Institutions of Credit to regulate transactions with those assets, issuing it's Circular 4/2019. Likewise, this Law established the need for accounting regulations, with which the Mexican Council for Financial Information Standards, AC, set a world precedent by being the first council to issue financial information standards (NIF) to create a specific standard worldwide. ; NIF C-22 "Cryptocurrencies" in force as of 2020. Likewise,

In the National Technical Committee for Comprehensive Risk Management of the Mexican Institute of Finance Executives, AC (IMEF), various risks are analyzed from a comprehensive perspective, including financial ones from the point of the volatility of the value of cryptocurrencies that, together with their The threat of increasing permissibility and the future possibility of naming commercial transactions in cryptocurrencies will generate a series of threats that financial executives must adequately monitor, evaluate and control.

It must be considered that there are other cryptocurrencies (LTC, XRP, DAI, ETH, GTN, BAT, BCH, MANA, TUSD, BAT) with different levels of transactionality and regulation, in some cases incipient, awaiting the emergence of others, which, will undoubtedly increase the associated financial risk. The IMEF has agreed with the world trends of technological threats, which adds risk to those already commented and related to cryptocurrencies given their virtual and technical nature. Cryptocurrencies are here to stay together with their risks, increased by the risk of their permissibility.

What does the automotive industry's future hold?

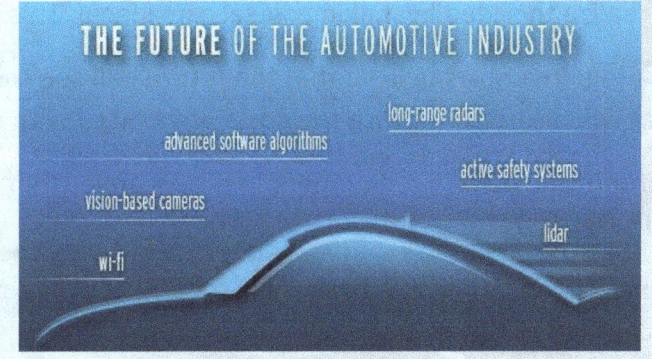

Karl Benz is credited with innovating the first gasoline-powered automobile among the many inventors of the 18th and 19th centuries.

It was a three-wheeled vehicle. An ingenious invention that hit the road 134 years ago. Back then, it was all about ease of movement, and while comfort was sought after, there was still room for improvement in innovation to give consumers what they were looking for.

Thanks to modern production methods, inventions that were once thought unlikely are now feasible a century later. The automotive industry is heavily digitalized today. It's no longer a matter of how but of when. It is now clear that revolutionary innovations are possible, and all that remains is for the inventors' concepts to be commercialized. Hardly a year goes by without an innovator building an idea because automakers subsequently adopt in their production, either in isolation or as part of a business strategy to boost sales.

The planet is undergoing a massive transformation, and technological advancement is at the heart of it. The auto industry is no exception. They are the biggest consumers of technology, who have made significant advances over the years. Autonomous driving is now an acceptable possibility; it's just a matter of who will implement it first. Prototypes have come out, with companies trying to outdo each other.

Car manufacturers have now acquired specific know-how, and their expertise in manufacturing is growing every day. The future of mobility is more linked to particular significant trends manifesting in the current digital age.

Current trends in the automotive sector

There is a great interest in these car manufacturers in satisfying the needs of the customers. They all align with the main vectors intended to shape the industry, namely autonomous driving, sharing, electrification, and connectivity. Through these critical megatrends, companies are transforming their manufacturing strategies to be relevant in the future.

The importance of these four elements

Electrification: Most countries are currently implementing legislation focused on manufacturing industries. They relate to vehicles that do not produce emissions. Some cities have already started to realize this idea by making diesel cars illegal. This initiative aims to reduce the carbon footprint.

Sharing: Inventors believe that the future will see the emergence of professionally managed fleets that will massively reduce the costs associated with mobility.

Autonomous: The development of automobiles that do not require human interaction but only use software to get around.

Connectivity: This will happen in different ways between cars, traffic infrastructure, and the occupants of those vehicles.

Innovative trends in the automotive industry are an exciting topic for any essay writer. There is no doubt that our mobility habits will change, and if you look at current trends, it already is. Compare the transportation trends of five or ten years ago to those of today. You will notice a significant change: widespread technological acceptance. The elements of communication and sharing represent it. There are numerous software-driven mobility solutions available, and people are more connected than ever before. It would have been impossible to imagine calling a taxi using an app twenty years ago, but it is now a reality.

Widespread adoption of software management tools

Software management tools have become synonymous for most companies, and companies in the automotive sector are also present. In the working environment of these companies, they allow better efficiency, which translates into easier management. Onboard vehicles, software management tools are implemented in different ways. Today, it's hard to spot a car that doesn't have comprehensive diagnostic software. These built-in tools primarily inform the car owner of an

underlying problem, and they also provide the capacity to control certain aspects of the vehicle digitally.

A definitive change in urban driving

Cities are multiplying, and now owning a car in large cities doesn't make as much sense as it once did, except when you have a reserved parking space, which is getting harder and harder to find. Today. Another disheartening aspect is that most motorists often find themselves in traffic jams, and that is demoralizing. People have started to change their lifestyles, and many are opting for less restrictive mobility solutions. The automakers have taken note of and are making the required adjustments.

There will be lesser car owners in large cities inevitably, and most people will opt for sharing. This way, many people can operate a single car which is probably powered by hydrogen or electricity. Of course, the future of the automotive industry holds some great surprises. Some significant trends have started to be widely adopted, and it is a matter of time before new trends emerge.

How is Cryptocurrency getting to the car without you noticing?

Although many do not yet know what Blockchain or how it is reaching the car, this is one of those words that have crawled into the day-to-day and is usually followed by the expressions' revolution' or 'it will change everything. Simplifying it a bit, Blockchain is a succession of encrypted records (hence, block, block in English) whose order cannot be altered (therefore, chain, chain in English) since they are not stored in a database to use. But in different nodes or users.

In this sense, there are two significant types of Blockchain networks for cars: closed (such as those already shared by some banks) or open (the most common example would be any of the already famous cryptocurrencies or tokens, such as Bitcoin). In either case, the key to the system is the existence of multiple users on that network since they are in charge of storing the blocks of data that are usually transactions but can record anything else.

Thus, every time you want to add new information to the chain, it must be validated by all or a large number of network users, making it impossible to alter it intentionally without anyone noticing. And this, obviously, also makes the Blockchain have multiple applications in the car.

Although many do not yet know what Blockchain or how it is reaching the car, this is one of those terms that has slipped into everyday use, typically accompanied by phrases like "revolution" or "it will change everything." Simplifying it a bit, Blockchain is a succession of encrypted records (hence, block, block in English) whose order cannot be altered (therefore, chain, chain in English) since they are not stored in a database to use. But in different nodes or users.

In this sense, there are two significant types of Blockchain networks for cars: closed (such as those already shared by some banks) or open (the most common example would be any of the already famous cryptocurrencies or tokens, such as Bitcoin). In either case, the key to the system is the existence of multiple users on that network since they are in charge of storing the blocks of data that are usually transactions but can record anything else.

Thus, every time you want to add new information to the chain, it must be validated by all or a large number of network users, making it impossible to alter it intentionally without anyone noticing. And this, obviously, also makes the Blockchain have multiple applications in the car.

And it is that, unlike a car, any Blockchain system is impossible to hack since for a pirate to break the security of Bitcoin, for example, he would have to access millions of computers simultaneously. For this reason, it is the banks that are adopting this technology the fastest, perhaps, because money, in reality, has already been traveling virtually for decades between the servers of financial institutions.

For the above, perhaps, it is an irony that the most famous of all the applications of this new technology, for now, are virtual coins or tokens such as Bitcoin. Many of them go hand in hand with business projects and, as happens like money itself, they go from symbolic value to real the more they are subject to strong demand and because their issuance is limited.

Adopting Blockchain in the car is closely related not to the technology or a particular app but also to create the most robust possible network. In this sense, the idea is that there will be a network of networks that intercommunicate all those not strictly private domains in the future.

Applications of the Blockchain to the automobile

Blockchain has reached the emergence of several phenomena: the connected car, Industry 4.0, and the data-driven economy. For car manufacturers, the Blockchain is an ideal way to interact with its hundreds of suppliers, since thanks to data chains, it is possible not only to know where and when

a part has been produced but also where its raw materials come from, who and how manufactured it, who transported it, under what conditions, etc. Your data has been stored in an open network of this technology, and you will be able to obtain all your history of owners or the repair one. There are already several projects that are creating the protocols for this, such as Verify Car.

Along the same lines, the Malaga company Moto block chain is creating digital records where motorcycle owners can record every euro spent on the maintenance of their vehicles and thus have a reliable tool for the buyer the day they put it on sale.

Cheaper car insurance thanks to Blockchain

Blockchain in Insurance: What to Expect?

Connectivity, in an environment of the future 5G for cars, together with this traceability of the Blockchain is also on the way to lead to the creation of car insurance that allows paying only for the amount or type of use made of the vehicle thanks to new smart contracts, with total reliability for both the user and the insurer.

Blockchain technology is already altering the way the car is used. Still, the data generated when driving is the vehicle's manufacturer vehicle manufacturer's property or the smartphone that goes in it. "This is going to change," says Irfon Watkins, creator of the startup Dovu, with a beta version of an app with which to be able to monetize the data you generate when traveling in tokens. "This information isn't going to make anybody rich, but in the future, you'll be able to securely pass it via Blockchain and be compensated in cryptocurrencies, which you can use to pay for things like parking."

Perhaps all this of the Blockchain and its applications in cars sounds as ethereal to you as the name of one of those famous cryptocurrencies, but, for example, Seat is already in the Spanish Alastria consortium, which brings together 70 of the largest companies in the country, constituted in a Blockchain network that also collaborates to explore solutions based on this technology for their common benefit.

In another consortium, Mobi, there are Bosch, Accenture, or universities like Berkeley to some governments with the so laudable 'leitmotif' of making smart mobility something safer and more efficient as cheap for the end-user. Manufacturers such as Honda and Renault are also in this initiative. But what is disruptive in this particular case is not only that this Blockchain for mobility consortium was born less than two years ago and that it already has more than 100 of these agents, but that access to its Blockchain will be 100% open. You and I can also be users.

As it happened with the Internet, Blockchain will bring enormous benefits for cars and people. Still, the speed at which its applications will become widespread will largely depend on the arrival of 5G, especially about the automobile. When the next phase of intelligent telephony is deployed, the connection speed will be 120 times higher than the current one. The autonomous car may be a reality and much of what we will do in the cabin. At the same time, we move without driving may be based on Blockchain technology.

"More than traceability, manufacturers should explore the possibilities of this technology to audit software updates. Some cars today have 100 million lines of code in their programming and when autonomous mobility spreads, the complexity of the programs and their updates will include decisions to life or death ", they remember from IBM. Hopefully, these decisions come as quickly as the future is.

The impact and future of cryptocurrencies

With the arrival of cryptocurrencies, the economy began to change, as they were presented as an alternative to the conventional system.

Cryptocurrencies continue in the eye of the hurricane. Although they have been on the market for several years and their use has increased over time, the truth is that their defenders are equal in number and passion to the detractors of the system. Among the latter are renowned economists and financial authorities who distrust their seriousness. They believe that because they are in a decentralized system that is not regulated by a public body, they can be lent for money laundering, finance illegal activities, or evade taxes. But let's go to a part of what cryptocurrencies are? They appear for the first time in 2008, during an economic crisis, when currencies from different countries faced a substantial devaluation, at a time when investments and capital also suffered strong blows. The creator of bitcoin, the digital currency par excellence, is Satoshi Nakamoto, a programmer who launches this virtual currency, which works on the Internet. Of course, it is not a physical currency but a system based on mathematics and cryptography, and which is made up of digits only.

And the truth is that we like it or not, with the arrival of cryptocurrencies, the economy began to change since they were presented as a brilliant alternative to the conventional system and had the attraction of not being subject to any central or public body: it works by supply and demand, is not linked to the formal financial system, to any central bank or a government.

All of the above also means that those who have invested and made their transactions in cryptocurrencies do not require intermediaries and therefore do not have to pay commissions. They make the transactions they want from their computer in a more agile and faster way, since -I insist- there are no intermediaries, rules, costs, fees, or anything like that. Then the transactions are done one by one, and each party has a virtual wallet from which the bitcoins are sent or received.

It is said that there are some 21 million bitcoin coins in circulation, although there are other virtual currencies, although less famous, among them ethereum, litecoin, and ripple. Experts predict that the daily use of bitcoin will grow by 363%, to 175,000 million in 2027, which means that it will become a third of the total of digital currencies. We keep asking ourselves, why so much attention on cryptocurrencies? For many reasons.

First, due to the high performance that bitcoin has achieved at times, and only during the last year it has achieved a considerable rise, just a few weeks ago, it had a substantial increase in its value, reaching more than the US $ 7,000 for one bitcoin. This has meant that investors try to get them anyway and that the financial system and the press put more interest there.

Without a doubt, this coin has established itself as a digital market leader. It has, however, experienced significant ups and downs, and it is difficult to predict whether it will rise or fall. As a result, we've come up with a list of other cryptocurrencies worth paying attention to.

Not everyone can trade in this market. Anyone who wants to buy, sell or issue a bitcoin must be an expert in technological and computational issues since it is a transaction that requires a higher technical level, understanding, and patience, as it is a complex and challenging task. Perhaps for the same reason, it has been pointed out that the programmers of this system have carried out and reviewed, through different mathematical algorithms, the system's security at the time of carrying out transactions.

Vital fact for the confidence of those who invest and buy or sell with cryptocurrencies.

With all the above, the call is to be attentive and be cautious. On the one hand, we have that there are already financial institutions that have already accepted these cryptocurrencies, such as Falcon Private Bank or Saxo Bank, which already has bitcoin on its trading platform. There are also large companies that have included it as a means of payment. . However, in the face of this boom, there are also voices that warn and affirm that it is a "possible bubble," so it is recommended to have some prudence when investing in them since they are still young currencies, which have arrived the minute they can experience the cost of being a system without any regulation.

Most likely, cryptocurrencies are here to stay. Without a doubt, it is still a system that needs time to establish itself and gain the trust of the vast majority. If they are going to play a relevant role in the world economy, only time will tell.

The ranking of the 10 most famous cryptocurrencies

1. Bitcoin (BTC)

Bitcoin is, without a doubt, the Cryptocurrency or Cryptocurrency for which you have learned the most. This digital currency's popularity stems from the fact that it was the first. It was founded in 2008 by a group of people going by the name Satoshi Nakamoto. Of course, it did not have the importance that it does now at the time of its initial release, and most people could not have predicted that it would achieve this level of data. Without a doubt, this coin has positioned itself as a leader in the digital market. It has, however, experienced significant ups and downs, and it is difficult to predict whether it will rise or fall. As a result, we've come up with a list of other cryptocurrencies worth paying attention to.

2. Ethereum (ETH)

Ethereum is not a currency, and it is a decentralized computing platform. We could represent it as a giant computer that is divided into multiple computers at the same time and works simultaneously. This computer network allows applications to be run on this distributed network, and operations are powered by the network's currency (ETH). The value of this Cryptocurrency reached all-time highs in February 2020, touching € 1,700 per ether.

3. Binance Coin (BNB)

Binance Coin is the company's official Cryptocurrency, a cryptocurrency exchange whose name is an acronym for "binary" and "finance." This Binance coin was born to support transactions within Binance's platform. In this vein, the Exchange's developers are attempting to raise the value of their tokens by launching Blockchain-related ventures that users can fund with Binance coins.

4. Cardano (ADA)

Cardano represents the so-called 3rd generation of the Blockchain that tries to solve the scalability problems typical of 2nd generation blockchains such as Etherium. Over the last few months, Cardano has become one of the fastest-growing assets in the entire cryptocurrency industry, multiplying its value more than 45 times in the previous year. Cardano is distinguished by using mathematical principles in its consensus mechanism and a unique multilayer architecture, making it stand out from other competing blockchains. With a team that participated in the creation of Ethereum, many are convinced that Cardano is the next generation of cryptocurrency solutions.

5. Tether (USDT)

Tether is a stablecoin or stable coin, which means that it is backed by an equal sum of standard fiat currencies like the dollar, euro, or Japanese yen.

Tether was explicitly designed to build the necessary bridge between fiat currencies and cryptocurrencies and offer stability, transparency, and minimal transaction fees to users.

Learn the basics of these new payment and financing methods to apply them within any business, It is attached to the US dollar and has a 1-to-1 ratio to the US dollar in terms of value. However, Tether Ltd. Makes no guarantee for any right to exchange or exchange Tethers for real money; that is, Tether cannot be exchanged for US dollars.

6. **Polkadot (DOT)**

We could define it as a Blockchain protocol that tries to connect the different existing blockchains to a universal blockchain. It is one of the biggest current problems of the Blockchain, the non-interoperability between the other chains (Bitcoin, Ethereum) Like most other blockchain infrastructure projects, Polkadot has its native token. The value of the DOT cryptocurrency has multiplied by more than 12 times in the last year, reaching highs in March 2021 worth € 33 per coin.

Unlike the rest of the platforms, Polkadot is among the newest and introduces a series of novel technical features to achieve its ambitious goal of encouraging the spread of cryptocurrencies. The DOT cryptocurrency plays a vital role in the maintenance and operation of the Polkadot network. By owning and wagering DOT, users gain the right to vote on network changes, and each vote corresponds to the amount of DOT crypto they own. That is what distinguishes this Cryptocurrency from others.

7. **Ripple (XRP)**

For many experts, Ripple (XRP) is the successor to Bitcoin since the original Bitcoin developers developed it to boost performance. Ripple's primary goal is to connect banks, payment providers, and digital asset exchanges, enabling faster and more profitable global payments. Like Bitcoin, Ripple is a secure and encrypted system whose transaction information is public, but payment information is not. In other words, it is a privileged system where the sender and receiver are the only ones who have the knowledge and the code that decrypts it.

8. **Uniswap (UNI)**

Uniswap is a complex software that runs on the Ethereum blockchain and allows decentralized swaps. Unicorns are used to make it functional (as its logo shows). At Uniswap, traders can trade Ethereum tokens without having to entrust their funds to anyone. At the same time, everyone can lend their crypto to liquidity pools, which are special reserves. In Exchange for providing money to these reserves, you will earn commissions. The Uniswap token has multiplied its value x10 in the last year, reaching historical highs of € 28.64 per token.

9. **Litecoin (LTC)**

Litecoin was introduced in 2011 as a Bitcoin substitute by former Google employee Charlie Lee. "People will buy stuff with Litecoin every day, in my opinion. It will clearly be the preferred mode of payment." It has a higher limit than Bitcoin, and there are currently about 60 million Litecoin in circulation. For this reason, many experts bet on this Cryptocurrency in the future.

10. **Chainlink (LINK)**

Chainlink is one of the most significant projects in the decentralized finance (Defi) ecosystem (LINK). It is a decentralized oracle service capable of providing external data to Ethereum smart contracts. In other words, it connects blockchains with the real world.

The token or the currency of this network (the LINK) multiplied its value x13 in the last year and reached historical highs in February at more than € 29 per coin.

The token of this network is the LINK, and it serves as an incentive for node operators to do a good job. Each of the installed nodes and the request for information correctly allows both the nodes and their operators to accumulate tokens as compensation.

Highlights: cryptocurrencies with a future

Last year we talked about news in cryptocurrencies or cryptocurrencies that to this day have not yet finished taking off, but which are worth taking into account. Not long ago, a report commented that the European Central Bank could look at some point issue crypto euros. A statement that named the advantages that the creation of this Cryptocurrency would entail.

Considering that currently, most of the money used in Europe is digitized in the form of a credit card. With a society accustomed to digital money, the appearance of this Cryptocurrency by the European Central Bank could reduce risks of insolvency in the entities and lower consumers' costs. This Cryptocurrency created in the United States pretends to be the substitute for the dollar. According to its creators, Fedcoin is the dream of all bankers because it would be a 100% international and digital currency. In addition, the most significant risks to the economy, which are bank runs and hyperinflation, could be eliminated at once.

How Blockchain will transform the auto industry and your care experience

Can you imagine a technology that allows the user to have control of their information, know how it is used, and be confident of the reliability and security of the data, as well as greater clarity in the communication processes with third parties? Learn the word well because there is the future: the Blockchain. Indeed, you have heard of bitcoins. As well? Cryptocurrencies are just one of the many requests for the Blockchain technology that underpins them. One of its primary uses is in transactions. However, the Blockchain is more than exchanging goods and services without intermediaries (such as banks).

While increasing the safety of procedures is one of its benefits, it can solve 187 everyday problems, according to Wired magazine. In this way, the Blockchain will revolutionize the markets and industries of the world since it will impact systems such as water supply, pensions, cancer, data protection, contracts, mortgage agreements, manufacturing processes and collection of industries, and even economic crises.

As a consequence, not only bureaucratic procedures can be streamlined from months to hours. One of its advantages is that it is straightforward to identify when a block has been altered, which would mean a scam attempt because any record connects to all the blocks.

And exactly how will it transform the auto industry?

Volkswagen Group is exploring the following uses:

- Assist in locking and unlocking the vehicle, even from a cell phone without being connected to the Internet, six times faster than current technology and more secure, thanks to efficient encrypted cryptography.
- The owner could authorize access to the car for a limited time to a third party.
- It would allow the safe handling of payment methods in parking lots, tolls, and energy billing after charging an electric car.

For example, a project in which Porsche is involved with eco-park aims to collect parking fees directly.

This means that the transaction is documented without the customer having to pay for parking on a machine. With the data that only Porsche knows, it will be possible to use services from other providers and then pay for them through Porsche without the need for intermediaries.

- Finally, another use would be to increase transparency in the supply chain, allowing intelligent monitoring of raw materials to know where each object is located along the entire chain.

While it sounds exceptional, Matthias Falkenberg, who designed the prototype of the parking fees, clarified that, although there is innumerable theoretical research on the subject, its wideranging practical use in the industry is still far away.

Even so, SEAT, for example, has joined the Alastria network to develop services and products based on this technology to improve the processes in the production and finance areas initially. In other words, the key to the future will be efficiency, transparency, speed, and security of movements and transactions of all kinds.

Blockchain is revolutionizing the automotive industry, and we will tell you how its implementation has been in the industry.

Security in the Blockchain, know the elements that make it up.

- **Fuel payment**

    In an era where cars will no longer depend on fossil fuels and will be 100 percent electric, it has been proposed as a possible and executable challenge to use the Blockchain so that the owner can make the advance payment of the vehicle load associated with the consumption. That you have had because as the entire system will be connected, the vehicle's loading will generate an amount of money to be disbursed that will be associated with your bank account. The idea of the project is to do the least amount of paperwork possible. For this, the Blockchain will record the consumption associated with the vehicle on average, but it is also expected that tax expenses such as parking and vehicle insurance are associated.

- **Autonomous data securely protected**

    The transit of vehicles is currently followed by satellite. Millions of companies have developed in this industry o ering tracking and location systems with security measures such as blocking through the VCM (Vehicle Control Module) module.

    Despite this, it has been repeatedly demonstrated that these systems are not 100% reliable, so transport companies such as Maersk bet on tracking through Blockchain networks. This is due to the reliability of the technology. In addition to this, data is currently being added to this tracking because it is no longer only essential to know where the vehicle is if it is on or if it exceeds the allowed speed. In this digitized world, more specific data is required, such as road conditions, real-time tra among other aspects that point to the near future, autonomous vehicles.

    For this, Big Data plays an important role, and the data that is stored in a blockchain network is reliable due to its inalterability, which also opens the possibility for OEMs to access this information safely and to be able to modify the manufacturing or improve it where appropriate, adapted to the real needs hosted on the network.

    General Motors Files Patent for Blockchain-Based Navigation Map

    It is a way that manufacturers can observe in a detailed and permanent form the resistance or efficiency of the products that are used in the construction of these vehicles, taking an essential role in the production chain. OEMs are the original manufacturing equipment; this means that they are the workforce of the brands; it is widespread in industries to have a quailed workforce dissociated from the brand.

- **Decentralized carpooling**

    The evolution of taxis is a reality, and UBER changed the model in which we made trips. Now we

    only access an application and ask for a driver to transfer us, we pay for the service, and that's it. We have stopped using our vehicles to use that of a third party, but at this point, there is a failure: we only change one way of using the service, but we have not changed the service itself. We depend on a third party that serves as a guarantor to connect the user with the driver. But multiple complaints have arisen over the arbitrary cancellation fees applied by the company. Currently, the blockchain projects promise to improve this system. Accurate and reliable way the cancellation fees, for example.

    In this sense, the user will not be asked arbitrarily, but a calculated and responsible way will be withheld a fee for the trip corresponding to the route traveled by the driver. In the same way, it is intended to use this type of technology to democratize this type of service, where users in a kind of pool set the rates taking into account particularities such as the comfort, mileage, and reputation of the drivers would promote the more conscious use of the service.

    Mercedes-Benz can monitor carbon emissions in the cobalt supply chain using Blockchain.

- **Carsharing**

    This innovative idea is currently used in Spain. A company with a set of electric vehicles has Implemented a carpool service. Through the Blockchain, they have created a network that

has allowed the integration of cars in principle with a mobile application. It will enable the vehicle's ignition, payment of rent, amount of parking, and payment of electric charge or fuel.

This idea was promoted from the statistics basically in the US, that there is overpopulation. This vehicle sharing system is an attractive option and solves mobility problems. It is encouraging not to purchase vehicles per adult but in a community way, thus negatively impacting the environment.

For this, the rental of this type of vehicle is encouraged at really low costs. The integration of blockchain technology in this particular has led to travel in a totally di erent and novel way. Something similar is being implemented in Argentina, but with ecological bicycles that depend on an application to access the use and return, the main difference is that it is free to use since it is financed by the government of the province of Buenas Aires. Siemens considers using blockchain technology for car sharing.

• **Tracking and supply**

Logically, large companies want to minimize fraud. For this, tracking in the parts supply chain is critical.

In the automotive industry, the security of traceability in part shipments is beginning to be used as something fundamental. Blockchain technology has already been used for some time by other sectors to guarantee the traceability of products. Still, as expected in an industry as large as the automotive sector, it has been successfully coupled to ensure that the parts, especially the electronic devices, are not Modi ed in any way from production to receipt of shipment of the details.

As expected, technological innovations take a while to be accepted. However, a decade has already been enough time to repeatedly demonstrate that the Blockchain really solves various problems and that its adaptability only requires invention by programmers.